ASIAN ICONOGRAPHY SERIES IV

Mother-Goddesses in Kathmandu

Musashi Tachikawa

ADROIT PUBLISHERS
DELHI-110 002

Published by
ADROIT PUBLISHERS
4675/21, Ganpati Bhawan, Ansari Road,
Daryaganj, New Delhi-110 002
Phones : 23266030, 23242552

Distributors
AKHIL BOOK DISTRIBUTORS
e-mail: akhilbooks@yahoo.com
akhilbooks@hotmail.com

ISBN : 81-87392-46-0

Layout
Sudhir Vatsa

Laser Typeset by
Nidhi Laser Point
e-mail: nidhi_vatsa@hotmail.com

Printed in India on behalf of M/s Adroit Publishers by
Arpit Printographers, B-7, Saraswati Complex,
Subhash Chowk, Laxmi Nagar, Delhi-110 092

PREFACE

This book presents iconographic studies of the Eight Mother-Goddesses *(mātṛkās)* in the Kathmandu Valley. The Kathmandu Valley contains over one thousand historical monuments and can be regarded as a huge museum. Niche-shrines, which house popular deities, are found in almost every corner of all the towns in the valley. Statues of Hindu or Buddhist deities are placed in front of the all prominent buildings or in the sanctuaries of temples. A number of religious images or icons can be seen on various parts of buildings such as walls and the tympanums *(toraṇa)* above the entrances. Statues are also found as part of the struts supporting the roofs. One could say that the Kathmandu Valley, including its three large cities: Kathmandu, Patan, and Bhaktapur, is inhabited by deities. People encounter divine images of icons around homes and wherever they go out within the valley. Moreover, the images of deities are even now-a-days used as the sacred symbols or paraphernalia of rituals, such as worship services to be observed in temples, or festivals to be performed throughout the whole city.

Although the national religion of Nepal is Hinduism, a considerable number of Buddhists are quite active in the Kathmandu Valley and the surrounding mountainous regions. Then there are Tibetans who have migrated from Central Tibet for several decades. They continue to try to preserve their own traditions in the city of Kathmandu as well as Patan. Some Newar Buddhists have to follow the Theravāda tradition without loosing their identity as Newars. Besides the great traditions of Buddhism and Hinduism, several small tribes observe their own cults in the Kathmandu Valley. Various religions which are closely related can be found in this valley. Two different religions, Buddhism and Hinduism, for example, sometimes share the same icons, or icons with similar features to a considerable degree. It often happens that Nepalese people identify a single image differently according to the religion to which they belong.

The iconography of Nepalese Hinduism is essentially the same as that of Indian Hinduism. There are, however, some important differences between them. One of the most important difference is that Nepalese Hinduism emphasizes the Eight Mātṛkās and the Eight Bhairavs. In the Kathmandu Valley one can find many temples which possess the relics or struts depicting the Eight Mātṛkās: Mahālakṣmī, Brahmāyaṇi (Skt., Brahmānī), Rudrāyaṇī (Skt., Rudrāni), Cāmuṇḍā, Kaumārī, Vaiṣṇavī, Indrāyaṇī (Skt., Indrāṇī), and Vārāhī.

Among the many shrines and temples in the Kathmandu Valley, I have chosen fifteen temples (or shrines) for this study, because they possess the images of the Eight Mātṛkās. Their images have been kept in good condition; the vehicles of the Mātṛkās can be clearly seen, and most of the symbols held in their hands have been preserved. These images can thus furnish materials for Hindu iconography in Nepal as well.

The struts depicting the Eight Mātṛkās are often placed together with the struts depicting the Eight Bhairavs: Asitāṅga, Ruru, Caṇḍa, Krodha, Unmatta, Kapāla, Bhīṣaṇa, and Saṃhāra. One can easily identify each of the Eight Mātṛkās by recognizing the vehicle, since each Mātṛkās is always mounted on the same type of vehicle. One cannot, however, identify each of the Eight Bhairavs in a similar manner. The vehicle of each of the Bhairavs is not consistent or determined, as it is in the case of a Mātṛkās. The symbols held in the hands of the Bhairavs are not helpful in identifying each Bhairav either.

First, I will briefly explain the structure and history of those temples and shrines I have chosen. Then I will illustrate the positions of the images of Mātṛkās and Bhairavs found in each shrine and temple.

This is a revised version of my papers entitled "Materials for Iconographic Studies of the Eight Mother-Goddesses in the Kathmandu Valley," Part I, Monumenta Serindica, No. 12; A.A. Institute, Tokyo, 1984, pp.1-122; Part 1-2, *ibid.*, 1985. pp. 41-116.

Musashi Tachikawa
Professor
National Museum of Ethnology
Osaka, Japan
July 8, 2003

CONTENTS

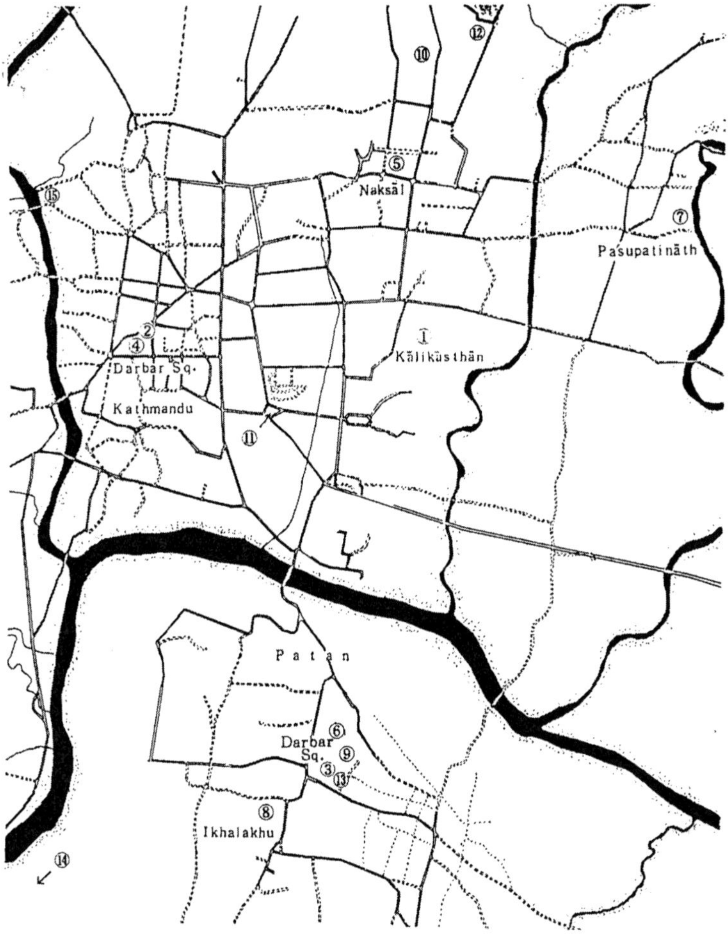

Map of Kathmandu and Patan

1. KĀLIKĀSTHĀN KĀLĪ TEMPLE[1)]

There is a temple of Goddess Kālī on the eastern edge of Kathmandu City. This area is called Kālīkāsthān, which literally means 'a Place of Kālī'. The shrine has been built on a base of about two meters in height, and towards the top of the temple there are four guilded snakes which support the crowning portion of the roof. There is no umbrella canopy on the top of it (Pl. 1). To the left of the temple there is a Pippala tree, under which there are a Śiva-liṅga, a trident, and stone images of Nandin, Bhairab with his consort, and Gaṇesh (Pl. 2).

In the centre of the temple, there is a niche-shrine of Goddess Kālī with a tympanum (*toraṇa*) that faces east and depicts the Eight Mātṛkās (Fig. 2; Pl. 3). Usually the Eight Mātṛkās are depicted on their vehicles, by which one can identify each Mātṛkā. Here, however, no vehicles are shown. Instead, the name of each Mātṛkā is inscribed at the bottom of each relief (Pl. 4-11).

Pl. 1	Kālikāsthān Kālī Temple
Pl. 2	Sacred images under a Pippala tree
Pl. 3	Kālī with the Eight Mātṛkās
Pl. 4	Mahālakṣmī
Pl. 5	Brahmāyaṇī
Pl. 6	Rudrāyaṇī
Pl. 7	Cāmuṇḍā
Pl. 8	Kaumārī
Pl. 9	Vaiṣṇavī
Pl. 10	Indrāyaṇī
Pl. 11	Vārāhī

Here the names:, Brahmāyaṇī, Rudrāyaṇī, and Indrāyaṇī are not used. Instead, the names: Brahmāyaṇī, Rudrāyaṇī, and Indrāyaṇī are inscribed.

Figure 1 Kālikāsthān Kāli Temple

2. TĀRAṆĪ DEVĪ TEMPLE[2)]

This single story temple is located to the north of the big Taleju Temple of Hanuman Dhoka, Kathmandu. The temple is dedicated to the Goddess Bhagavatī (Pl. 12) and is supported by Śāktas. According to *KV*, the figure carved on the central tympanum, who is mounted on a lion, is Vaiṣṇavī[3)] Vaishṇavī is, however, usually mounted on Garuḍa (Pl. 13).

The struts on the front-side of the building present the Eight Mātṛkās, Śiva, and Bhairab (Fig. 2). Each deity is depicted as mounted on her or his own vehicle. Kaumārī is depicted as mounted on a peacock (Pl.14); Vārāhī, on buffalos (Pl.15)[4)] Brahmāyaṇī, on geese (Pl.16); Rudrāyaṇī or Durgā, on lions (Pl.17)[5)]; Vaiṣṇavī, on Garuḍas (Pl.18); Indrāyaṇī, on elephants (Pl. 19); Mahālakṣmī, on lions (Pl. 20); Śiva, on bulls (Pl. 21); Cāmuṇḍā, on a human corpse (Pl. 22); and Bhairab, on a lion (Pl. 23)[6] The image depicted on the fourth strut from the right of the central tympanum is being offered a pair of buffalo's horns, which are often offered to Durgā or Rudrāyaṇī (Pl.17).

Pl. 12 Tāraṇī Devī Temple
Pl. 13 Bhagavatī depicted on the central tympanum
Pl. 14 Kaumārī
Pl. 15 Vārāhī
Pl. 16 Brahmāyaṇī
Pl. 17 Rudrāyaṇī
Pl. 18 Vaiṣṇavī
Pl. 19 Indrāyaṇī
Pl. 20 Mahālakṣmī
Pl. 21 Śiva
Pl. 22 Cāmuṇḍā
Pl. 23 Bhairab

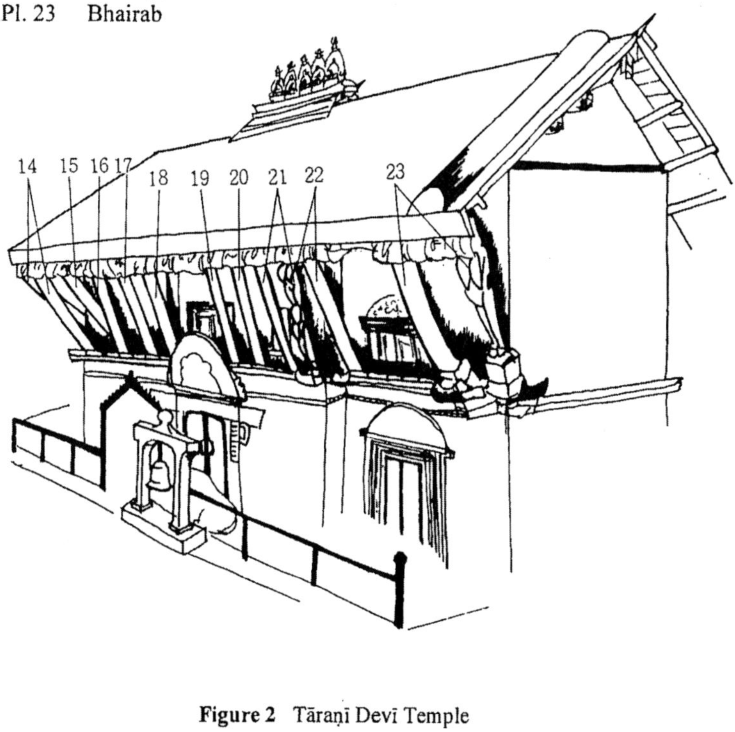

Figure 2 Tāraṇī Devī Temple

3. THE WESTERN FACADE OF THE MŪL CHOWK, PATAN[7)]

The western facade of the Mūl Chowk (Main Court) facing Darbar Square in Patan, possesses struts depicting the Eight Mātṛkās and the Eight Bhairabs (Fig. 3; Pl. 24). On the roof of the Mūl Chowk is a small square-shaped temple. It is the small Taleju Temple, where Malla's tutelary goddess is enshrined.

Pl. 24 The western facade of the Mūl Chowk

[The following twenty deities are depicted on the struts supporting the western roof of the Mūl Chowk (Fig. 3; Pl. 25-44). The four deities shown in Plates 33-36 are neither Mātṛkās nor Bhairabs.]

Pl. 25 A Bhairab mounted on a human being
Pl. 26 Brahmāyaṇī
Pl. 27 A Bhairab mounted on a dog
Pl. 28 Rudrāyaṇī
Pl. 29 A Bhairab mounted on a boar
Pl. 30 Kaumārī
Pl. 31 A Bhairab mounted on Garuḍa
Pl. 32 Vaiṣṇavī
Pl. 33 Unidentified
Pl. 34 Unidentified
Pl. 35 Unidentified
Pl. 36 Unidentified
Pl. 37 A Bhairab mounted on a snake
Pl. 38 Vārāhī
Pl. 39 A Bhairab (His vehicle is unidentified.)
Pl. 40 Indrāyaṇī
Pl. 41 A Bhairab mounted on a horse
Pl. 42 Cāmuṇḍā
Pl. 43 A Bhairab mounted on a human being
Pl. 44 Mahālakṣmī
Pl. 45 A strut depicting a rampant lion

[The following deity is depicted on the strut which is to the right of the rampant lion shown in Pl. 45.]

Pl. 46 Kumāra

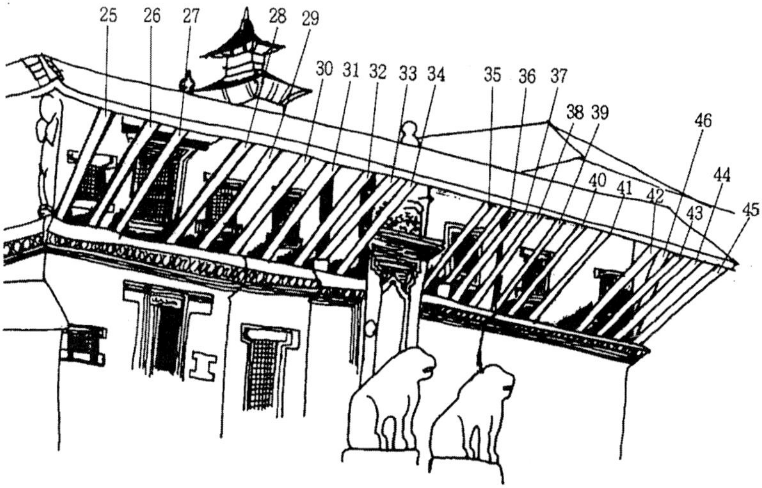

Figure 3 The western facade of the Mūl Chowk

4. KĀL BHAIRAB SHRINE[8)]

This open shrine of Kāl Bhairab was constructed in 1660. According to a legend, the huge stone image of Kāl Bhairab was found near Raniban where Pratāpa Malla was constructing the Bhandarkhal Gardens. At the both sides of the main image, there is a panel of the Eight Mātṛkās and Śiva.

Pl. 47 Kāl Bhairab Shrine
Pl. 48 Two images of Umāmaheśvara
Pl. 49 Śiva

[The following Mātṛkās are depicted on the panel (Pl. 50-53).]

Pl. 50 Brahmāyaṇī (right) and Maheśvarī (left)
Pl. 51 Kaumārī (right) and Vaiṣṇavī (left)
Pl. 52 Vārāhī (right) and Mahālakṣmī (left)
Pl. 53 Cāmuṇḍā (right) and Indrāyaṇī (left)
Pl. 54 Umāmaheśvara

Figure 4 Kāl Bhairab Shrine

5. NAKSĀL BHAGAVATĪ TEMPLE[9)]

This Śākta temple is situated in Bhagavatī Vahāl of Naksāl. The three-storied main building of this temple is a good example of Nepalese pagoda-shaped temples. On either side of the main entrance of the building, there are a lion and a Nāgī. The main deity of this temple is a goddess who is depicted as slaying a buffalo demon. The idol is depicted on a tympanum at the main entrance. Elaborately carved struts support the guilded roofs, and there is a *kiṅkinimālā* (metal border) on all the roofs. Four flags are suspended from the lowest roof, and figures of birds are placed on all four corners of the upper two roofs. The pinnacle is rather simple, and has a floral umbrella.[10)] It is, however, characteristic of this temple to have frescoes on all four walls of the first floor,[11)] which depict Śiva in various forms, his consorts, and his attendants such as a *khyāk* (Skt., *bhūta*, a spirit of the dead).

The exact construction-date of the main building of this temple is unknown. According to records, this temple was renovated in 1781. However, the divine image of the goddess slaying the buffalo demon, which is enshrined in the sanctuary of this temple, is surprisingly old. It is considered to have been made in the twelfth or thirteenth century.[12)] The struts supporting the lowest roof have carvings of the Eight Mātṛkās and the Eight Bhairabs[13)] (Pl.

69-84). The four struts supporting the southern middle roof show Śiva's family: Gaṇesh who is Śiva's son (Pl. 86), Śiva (Pl. 87), Pārvatī who is Śiva's consort (Pl. 88), and Kumāra, another son of Śiva(Pl. 89).

Pl. 55 Naksāl Bhagavatī Temple
Pl. 56 The tympanum of the entrance, depicting the Goddess Mahiṣāsuramardinī
Pl. 57 The image of Mahiṣāsuramardinī placed in the sanctuary of the temple

[The following deities are depicted on the frescoes of the four walls of the main building (Pl. 58-68).]

Pl. 58 Śiva disguided as a *khyāk*, and a skeleton demon (*kaṅkāla*)
Pl. 59 *Khyāks*
Pl. 60 Śiva
Pl. 61 Śiva receiving the stream of the Gaṅgā on his head
Pl. 62 Kumāra (?)
Pl. 63 A skeleton-demon
Pl. 64 Maheśvarī
Pl. 65 Śiva disguised as a *khyāk*
Pl. 66 A *khyāk*
Pl. 67 Mahālakṣmī
Pl. 68 A *khyāk*

[The following deities are the Eight Mātṛkās and the Eight Bhairabs depicted on the sixteen struts supporting the lowest roof (Fig. 5; Pl. 69-85).]

Pl. 69 A Bhairab mounted on a lion
Pl. 70 Kaumārī
Pl. 71 A Bhairab (His vehicle is unidentified.)
Pl. 72 Maheśvarī
Pl. 73 A Bhairab (His vehicle is probably a boar.)
Pl. 74 Brahmāyaṇī
Pl. 75 A Bhairab mounted on Garuḍa
Pl. 76 Indrāyaṇī
Pl. 77 A Bhairab mounted on a dog
Pl. 78 Vaiṣṇavī
Pl. 79 A Bhairab mounted on a human being
Pl. 80 Mahālakṣmī

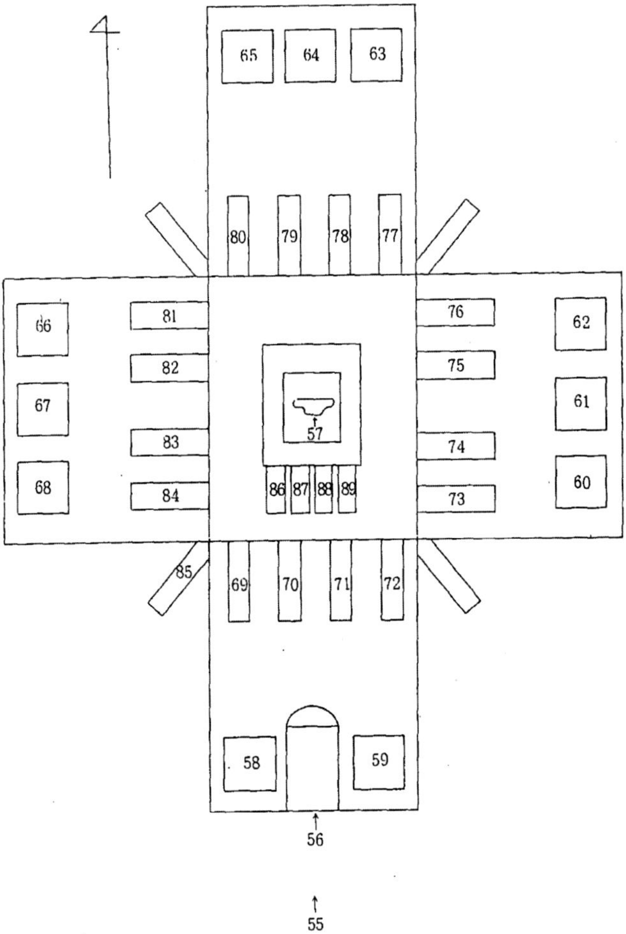

Figure 5 Naksāl Bhagavatī Temple

Pl. 81 A Bhairab mounted on a horse
Pl. 82 Vārāhī
Pl. 83 A Bhairab mounted on a snake
Pl. 84 Cāmuṇḍā
Pl. 85 A strut depicting a rampant lion

[The following four deities are depicted on the four struts supporting the southern part of the middle roof of the three-storied temple (Pl. 86-89).]

Pl. 86 Gaṇesh, who is Śiva's the first son of Śiva.
Pl. 87 Śiva
Pl. 88 Maheśvarī, who is Śiva's consort
Pl. 89 Kumāra, who is the second son of Śiva.

6. BHELACHHEN ULMANTA BHAIRAB TEMPLE[14)]

This three-storied temple is located in Bhelachhen, which is to the north of Darbar Square in Patan. This temple is dedicated to Mahābhairab, and belongs to the Śiva sect as well as the Śākta sect. Records show that the temple was built in 1541. On the sixteen struts supporting the lowest roof of the temple are statues of the Eight Mātṛkās and the Eight Bhairabs.

Pl. 90 Bhelachhen Ulmanta Bhairab Temple
Pl. 91 The entrance to the sanctuary of the temple
Pl. 92 Bhairab depicted on the tympanum above the entrance (detail of Pl. 91)
Pl. 93 The struts supporting the lowest roof (In this plate one can see horns of buffalos, which have been offered to the deity enshrined in this temple.)

[The following sixteen deities are the Eight Mātṛkās and the Eight Bhairabs depicted on the sixteen struts supporting the lowest roof of the temple (Pl. 94-109).[15)]]

Pl. 94 Ruru Bhairab mounted on a human being
Pl. 95 Maheśvarī
Pl. 96 Ulmanta Bhairab mounted on a lion
Pl. 97 Brahmāyaṇī
Pl. 98 A Bhairab mounted on a human being
Pl. 99 Mahālakṣmī

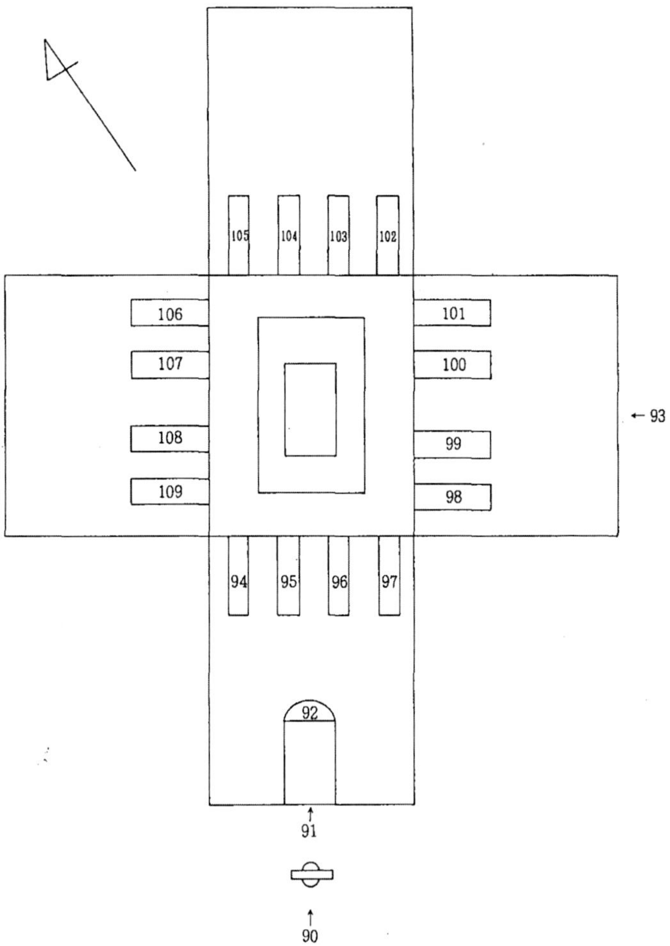

Figure 6 Bhelachhen Ulmanta Bhairab Temple

Pl. 100 A Bhairab mounted on a horse
Pl. 101 Cāmuṇḍā
Pl. 102 Asitāṅga Bhairab mounted on a bull
Pl. 103 Indrāyaṇī
Pl. 104 Kapāla Bhairab mounted on a snake
Pl. 105 Vārāhī
Pl. 106 A Bhairab mounted on Garuḍa
Pl. 107 Vaiṣṇavī
Pl. 108 Pracaṇḍa Bhairab mounted on a boar
Pl. 109 Kaumārī

7. BACHHARESHWARĪ TEMPLE[16)]

This pagoda-style temple is located on the bank of the Bagmati River. It is a two-storied temple of about six meters in height. There are not any idols inside of the temple, there remains only a small, round base made of stone.[17)] On the eight struts supporting the lower roof are statues of the Eight Bhairabs; on the eight struts of the upper roof of the temple are the Eight Mātṛkās. On the four walls of the first story are paintings of *kaṅkālas* and *bhūtas*. Evidently some struts depicting Bhairabs are rather new. This temple is also called the Pārvatī Temple. Plates 111-118 show the images of the Eight Mātṛkās which are found on the struts of the upper roofs. Although their symbols can not be clearly observed, one can tell the name of each Mātṛkā by the vehicle.

Pl. 110 Bachhareshvarī Temple

[The following Eight Mātrkās are on the eight struts supporting the upper roof of the temple (Pl. 111-119).]

Pl. 111 Vārāhī
Pl. 112 Cāmuṇḍā
Pl. 113 Indrāyaṇī
Pl. 114 Brahmāyaṇī
Pl. 115 Mahālakṣmī (She might be Maheśvarī.)
Pl. 116 Maheśvarī (She might be Mahālakṣmī.)
Pl. 117 Vaiṣṇavī
Pl. 118 Kaumārī
Pl. 119 A strut depicting a rampant lion

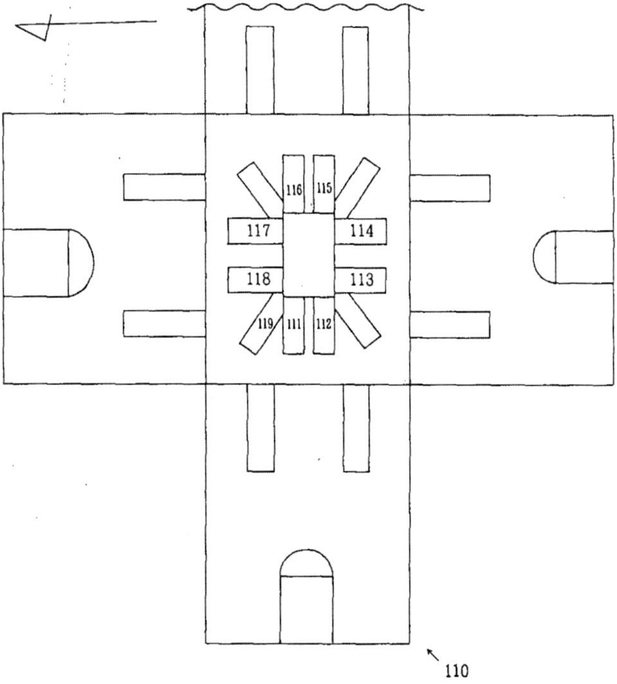

Figure 7 Bachhareshwarī Temple

8. IKHALAKHU BHAIRAB TEMPLE[18]

This temple is located at Ikhalakhu, near Darbar Square in Patan. It was constructed in 1727, and was renovated in 1904. The deity enshrined in this temple is supposedly Bhairab. The temple is supported by Hindus and Buddhists as well. The sixteen struts supporting the lower roof show the Eight Mātṛkās and the Eight Bhairabs. See in Fig. 8.

Pl. 120 Ikhalakhu Bhairab Temple
Pl. 121 The entrance of the temple (The southern facade depicts a skeleton-demon and a *khyāk*.)

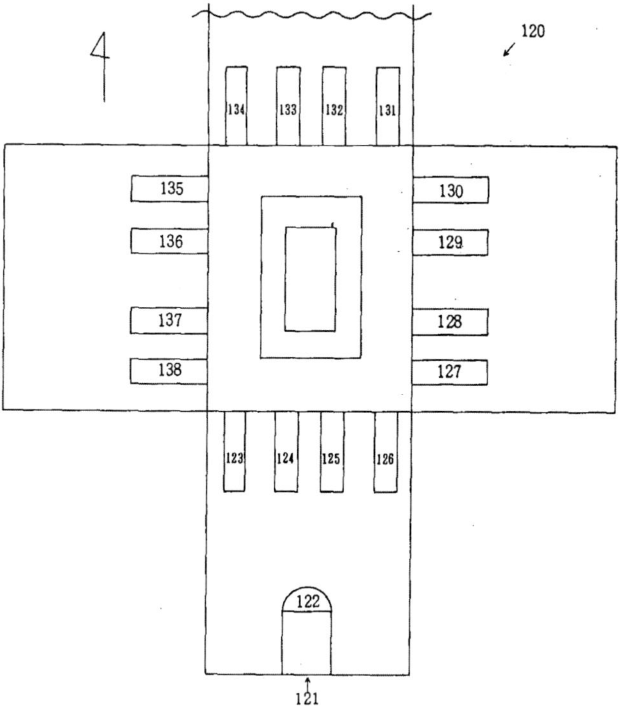

Figure 8 Ikhalakhu Bhairab Temple

Pl. 122 The tympanum depicting Bhairab, the deity enshrined in this temple (detail of Pl. 121).

[The following sixteen deities are depicted on the sixteen struts supporting the lowest roof of the temple (Pl. 123-138).]

Pl. 123 A Bhairab mounted on Garuḍa
Pl. 124 Vaiṣṇavī
Pl. 125 A Bhairab mounted on a bull (?)
Pl. 126 Kaumārī
Pl. 127 A Bhairab mounted on a dog

Pl. 128 Maheśvarī
Pl. 129 A Bhairab mounted on a lion
Pl. 130 Brahmāyaṇī
Pl. 131 A Bhirab mounted on a human being
Pl. 132 Mahālakṣmī
Pl. 133 A Bhairab mounted on a horse
Pl. 134 Cāmuṇḍā
Pl. 135 A Bhairab mounted on a bull
Pl. 136 Indrāyaṇī
Pl. 137 A Bhairab mounted on a snake
Pl. 138 Vārāhī

9. OLAKHU GAṆESH TEMPLE[19)]

This three-storied temple in located in Olakhu, Patan. It is dedicated to the Deity Jor Gaṇesh. This temple is considered as sacred by Buddhists, Śaivites, Śāktas, and Vaiṣṇavites. In front of the temple, there are images of a rat (which is the vehicle of Gaṇesh), a bell, and two guardian lions (Pl. 139). An image of Gaṇesh is on the tympanum above the entrance (Pl. 140). Eight Mātṛkās and Eight Bhairabs (Pl. 142-157) can be seen on the sixteen struts supporting the lowest roof. According to the inscription, the upper stories were built in 1684, and the struts in 1681 (Pl. 158-161).[20)]

Pl. 139 Olakhu Gaṇesh Temple
Pl. 140 The tympanum above the entrance, which depicts Gaṇesh
Pl. 141 A Gaṇesh image inside the sanctuary of the temple

[The following sixteen deities are the Eight Mātṛkās and the Eight Bhairabs depicted on the sixteen struts supporting the lowest roof of the temple (Pl. 142-157).]

Pl. 142 A Bhairab mounted on a lion
Pl. 143 Brahmāyaṇī
Pl. 144 A Bhairab mounted on a human being
Pl. 145 Mahālakṣmī
Pl. 146 A Bhairab mounted on a horse
Pl. 147 Cāmuṇḍā
Pl. 148 A Bhairab mounted on a bull
Pl. 149 Indrāyaṇī

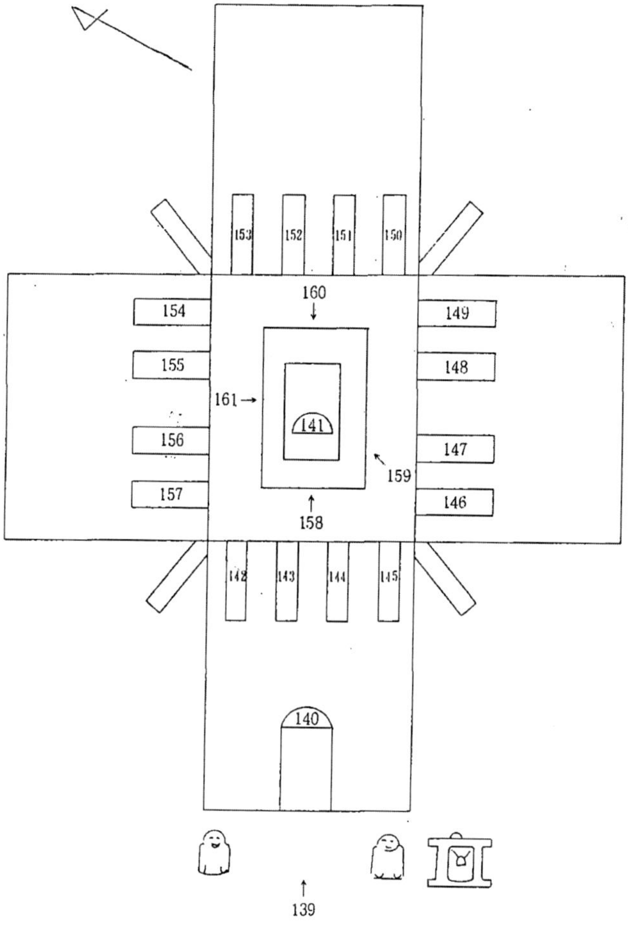

Figure 9 Olakhu Gaṇesh Temple

Pl. 150 A Bhairab mounted on a snake
Pl. 151 Vārāhī
Pl. 152 A Bhairab mounted on Garuḍa
Pl. 153 Vaiṣṇavī
Pl. 154 A Bhairab mounted on a boar
Pl. 155 Kaumārī
Pl. 156 A Bhairab mounted on a dog
Pl. 157 Maheśvarī
Pl. 158 The struts supporting the south-western roofs of the temple
Pl. 159 The struts supporting the south-eastern roofs of the temple
Pl. 160 The struts supporting the north-eastern roofs of the temple
Pl. 161 The struts supporting the north-western roofs of the temple

10. BHĀṬBHAṬENĪ TEMPLE[21)]

This two-storied temple is located at Tangal, on the northern outskirts of Kathmandu City. The facades of this temple are covered by glazed tiles. Along the walls of the second story, there are drawings of household utensils such as water pots and saucepans, offered to gods when the wishes of worshippers have been granted (Pl. 162). On the tympanum at the entrance, which faces north, there is an image of a goddess, which is believed by locals to be enshrined in this temple. Its name is Bhaṭenī, and she is also considered to be an incarnation of Brahmāyaṇī.

In front of the northern facade, there are a number of temple accessories, such as bells, flags, and lamp stands (Pl. 164). On the four facades of the temple are the images of Mātṛkās, Gaṇesh, Kumāra, and *khyāks* (Pl. 164-177). An iguana, which is often associated with goddesses (Pl. 179),[22)] is also depicted on each strut supporting the lower roof.

A Brahman couple, Bhāṭ and Bhaṭenī, are enshrined in this temple. They were said to have established it near by the town called Bisalnagar. Legend tells that they were devoted to Viṣṇu, and that when their son was carried away by a huge kite (which was Garuḍa, Viṣṇu's vehicle), Viṣṇu consoled them. People in this area believe that the two divinities are capable of curing the diseases of children. The life-sized images of the couple and their son altogether hang from the ceiling of the temple's main sanctuary.

Pl. 162 Bhāṭbhaṭenī Temple (northern and eastern facades)
Pl. 163 On the tymanum at the entrance, an image of Brahmāyaṇī
Pl. 164 The northern facade and the entrance of the temple

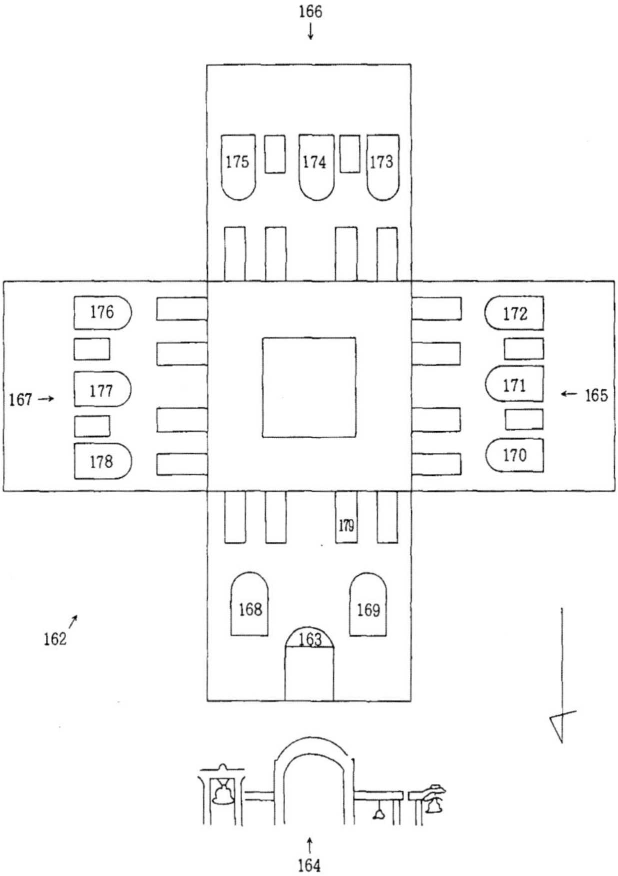

Figure 10 Bhāṭbhaṭenī Temple

Pl. 165 The western facade with the frescoes depicting Indrāyaṇī (cf. Pl. 170), Vaiṣṇavī (cf. Pl. 171), Vārāhī (cf. Pl. 172)

Pl. 166 The southern facade with the frescoes depicting Dakṣṇakālī (cf. Pl. 173), Bhaṭenī (cf. Pl. 174), Gaṇesh (cf. Pl. 175)

Pl. 167 The eastern facade with the frescoes depicting Maheśvarī (cf. Pl. 176), Mahālakṣmī (cf. Pl. 177), Kumāra (cf. Pl. 178)

[The following twelve images are painted in the frescoes of the four facades (Pl. 168-178).]

Pl. 168 Gaṇesh
Pl. 169 Kumāra
Pl. 170 Indrāyaṇī
Pl. 171 Vaiṣṇavī
Pl. 172 Vārāhī
Pl. 173 Dakṣṇakālī
Pl. 174 Bhaṭenī, who is identified with Brahmayāṇī (cf. Pl. 163)
Pl. 175 Gaṇesh
Pl. 176 Maheśvarī
Pl. 177 Mahālakṣmī
Pl. 178 Kumāra
Pl. 179 An iguana

11. BHADRA KĀLĪ TEMPLE[23)]

This temple is situated between Tundikhel and Singh Durbar. The goddess of this temple is known as Lumari ('Gold-bread') or Ludadī Devī ('Gold-giving-goddess'). A Newar legend has it that in ancient times, the bread of a farmer was transformed into gold through the power of this goddess. The Newari word '*lu*' means gold; '*mari*,' bread.[24)]

Pl. 180 shows the main shrine of the temple. A niche-shrine similar to the one at Kālikāsthān Temple, is in this temple (cf. Pl. 3). Goddess Cāmuṇḍā is also known by the name of Bhadra Kālī or Kāralī, when she has eight arms.[25)] The main deity of this temple is eight-armed Bhadra Kālī, and is depicted on the top of the niche-shrine (Pl. 182). There is no image of Bhadra Kālī at the base of the niche-shrine. Only a small, round, metallic cover symbolizes Bhadra Kālī. It is situated in the tantric fashion (Pl. 181).

Pl. 183 shows the reverse side of the temple altar. A large metallic canopy is above it. Pl. 184 shows the image of Bhadra Kālī that is shown in Pl. 183.

The Eight Mātṛkās, together with the eight auspicious signs, are depicted on the metallic canopy placed above the *toraṇa* (Pl. 185). There is a relief of Bhadra Kālī in the center of the canopy (Pl. 186).

The Eight Mātṛkās are arranged in the following order (cf. Fig.12).

Pl. 187 Brahmāṇī ········ west
Pl. 188 Rudrāṇī ········ south-west
Pl. 189 Kaumārī ········ south
Pl. 190 Vaiṣṇavī ········ south-east
Pl. 191 Vārāhī ········ east
Pl. 192 Indrāṇī ········ north-east
Pl. 193 Cāmuṇḍā ········ north
Pl. 194 Mahālakṣmī ········ north-west

Idols of deities such as Viṣṇu, Kumāra, and Gaṇesh, carved out of natural stones, have been stored in the main shrine of Bhadra Kālī Temple (cf. Fig. 11). Pl. 195 shows the stone symbolizing Vārāhī. Aboriginal female deities (*ajima*) are often symbolized by a carving on a stone plate (Pl. 196).

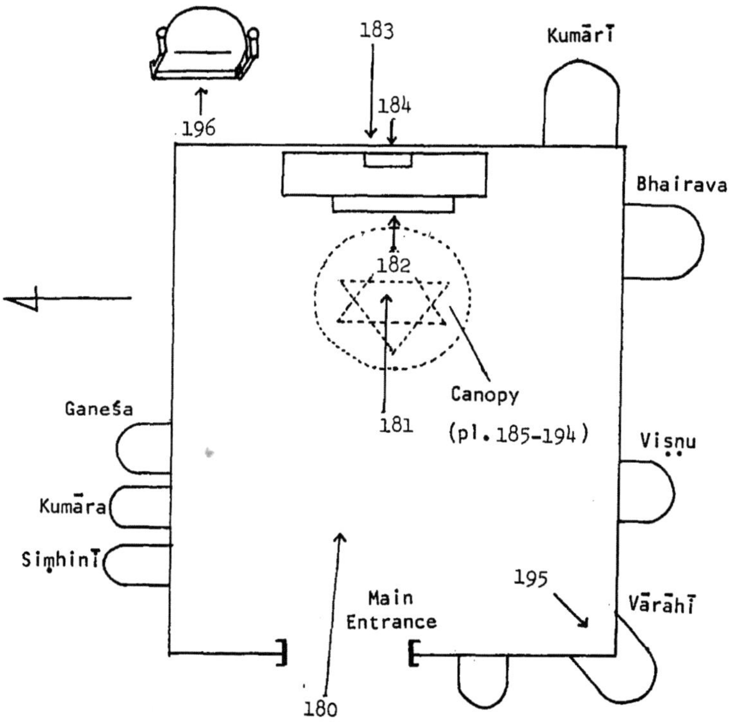

Figure 11 Bhadra Kālī Temple

Figure 12 The Canopy of Bhadra Kālī Temple

12. HADIGAON BHAGAVATĪ TEMPLE[26)]

This small temple was constructed in the eighteenth century and is situated in the northern part of Kathmandu City. As one can judge from the name of the temple, it belongs to the Śākta sect. But an image of Kārttikeya, Śiva's son, has been installed in the center of the sanctuary of the temple.[27)] He is six-faced and twelve-armed. He is seen being mounted on a *garuḍa*, which is the vehicle of Viṣṇu. His arms hold a number of weapons including a *cakra*, a *vajra*, and a trident, which are originally the weapons of Viṣṇu, Indra, and Śiva.

In front of the main entrance of Hadigaon Bhagavatī Temple, the Navagrahas (the Sun, Moon, Mercury, Venus, Mars, Jupiter, Saturn, Rāhu, and Ketu) are symbolized by nine small circles carved on a small stone plate (cf. Fig. 13). Near the plate there is an image of Umāmaheśvara (Goddess Umā and her husband, Maheśvara. Pl. 199).

Pl. 197 Hadigaon Bhagavatī Temple
Pl. 198 Kārttikeya mounted on a *garuḍa*
Pl. 199 Umāmaheśvara

The eight struts, supporting the lower roof of the two-storied temple, depict the Eight Mātṛkās.

Pl. 200 Indrāṇī
Pl. 201 Vārāhī
Pl. 202 Vaiṣṇavī
Pl. 203 Kaumārī
Pl. 204 Rudrāṇī
Pl. 205 Brahmāṇī
Pl. 206 Mahālakṣmī
Pl. 207 Cāmuṇḍā

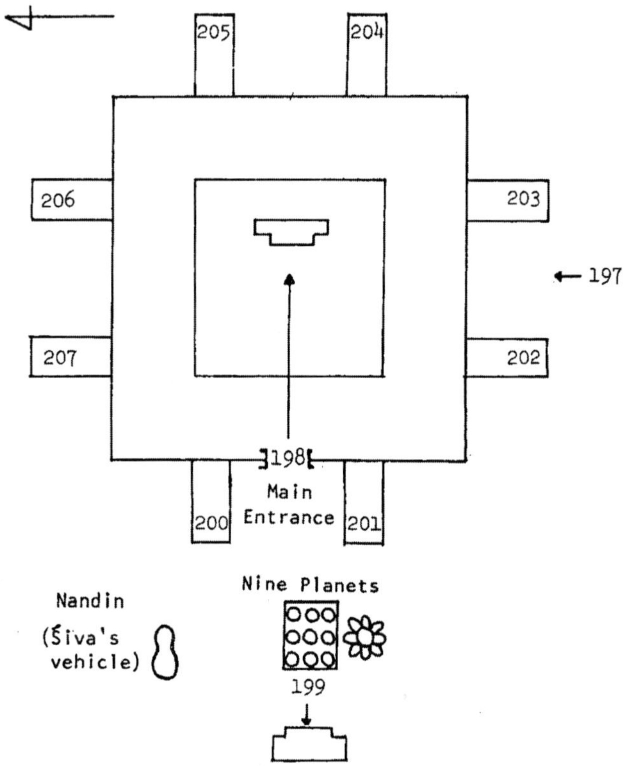

Figure 13 Hadigaon Bhagavatī Temple

13. THE COURTYARD OF THE MŪL CHOWK IN PATAN[28)]

The Mūl Chowk, which was constructed in the seventeenth century, is a part of the old royal palace of Patan. It was used as one of the most important sites for the rituals conducted by the Patan kings. The buildings of the Mūl Chowk were designed in such a way that four wings enclose a regular square courtyard. The famous Small Taleju Temple is located on the roof of the south wing of the Mūl Chowk (cf. Fig.3).[29)] This pagoda-style temple is square and three-storied. The entrance to the Small Taleju Temple is below the temple located on the ground level. The Small Taleju Temple has a *toraṇa*, but the deity-images are missing there (Pl. 208). Below the *toraṇa*, there is a small relief showing Goddess Cāmuṇḍā who is probably identified with Goddess Taleju (Pl. 210).

Surround the courtyard, the roofs of the Mūl Chowk are held up by a number of struts with Hindu deities. The deities are presented in a stance suggesting they wish to watch the humans performing the rituals or to watch animals being sacrificed in the courtyard (Pl. 209). The Eight Mātṛkās, Durgā, and Bhairavas (or Bhairabs) are depicted on the struts supporting the western roof and on one strut supporting the southern roof of the Mūl Chowk (Pl. 211-226).

Pl. 208 The entrance to the Small Taleju Temple (Intestines of a sacrificed animal is hanging over the small square relief of Cāmuṇḍā and plays the role of a flower garland.)

Pl. 209 Struts depicting Mātṛkās and Bhairabs (From left to right of the photo, Brahmāṇī (cf. Pl. 214), a Bhairab mounted on a dog (cf. Pl. 215), Rudrāṇī (cf. Pl. 216), and a Bhairab mounted on a boar (cf. Pl. 217).)

Pl. 210 A small square relief Cāmuṇḍā which is attached to the top of the entrance of the Small Taleju Temple (cf. Pl. 208)

Pl. 211 A strut depicting Mahālakṣmī supports the edge of the southern roof of the Mūl Chowk.

Pl. 212 A strut depicting Durgā supports the edge of the western roof of the Mūl Chowk.

Pl. 213 A Bhairab mounted on a *preta* or a human being

Pl. 214 Brahmāṇī

Pl. 215 A Bhairab mounted on a dog

Pl. 216 Rudrāṇī

Pl. 217 A Bhairab mounted on a boar

Pl. 218 Kaumārī

Pl. 219 A Bhairab mounted on a *garuḍa*

Pl. 220 Vaiṣṇavī

Pl. 221 A Bhairab mounted on a snake

Pl. 222 Vārāhī

Pl. 223 A Bhairab mounted on a bull

Pl. 224 Indrāṇī

Pl. 225 A Bhairab mounted on a horse

Pl. 226 Cāmuṇḍā

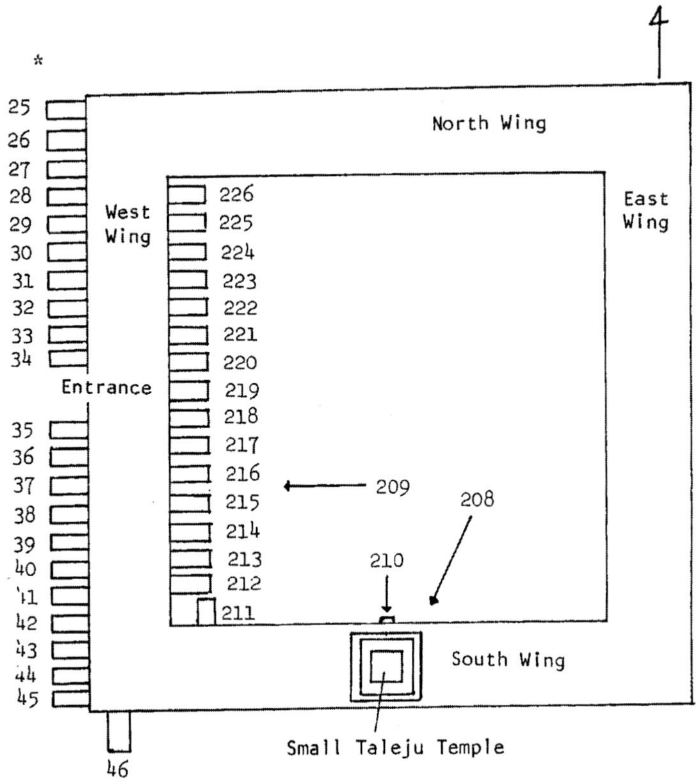

Figure 14 The Courtyard of the Mūl Chowk in Patan

14. DAKṢIṆA KĀLĪ TEMPLE[30)]

This Kālī temple is located in the southern part of the Kathmandu Valley near the Bāgmati River. There is another Dakṣiṇa Kālī temple in Thamel, which is in the northern sector of Kathmandu City.[31)] These two temples are not, however, affiliated with each other. "Dakṣiṇa Kālī" means goddess named Kālī which faces south (*dakṣiṇa*), a direction which is considered inauspicious and impure. Ancient Indians believed that the spirits of the dead go to the south and stay there; so most images of Hindu deities do not face south. Among the various kinds of goddesses called "Kālī," the Dakṣiṇa Kālī is especially terrifying and hideous. The Dakṣiṇa Kālī cult has continued prevailing not only in Nepal, but also in eastern India.

The site of the Kālī temple in the southern part of the Kathmandu Valley dates back to the fourteenth century. The buildings of the temple are situated on a small peninsula created by the convergence of two streams (Pl. 227). In front of the temple altar there are images of the Goddess Dakṣiṇa Kālī, the Seven Mātṛkās, and Gaṇeśa or Gaṇesh (Pl. 228-229). Animal sacrifices are performed at this temple every week, and the blood of the sacrificed animals is poured upon the images of the Dakṣiṇa Kālī and the Mātṛkās.

Pl. 227 Dakṣiṇa Kālī Temple
Pl. 228 Dakṣiṇa Kālī, Cāmuṇḍā, Indrāṇī, Vārāhī, and Vaiṣṇavī (from left to right)
Pl.229 Kaumārī, Rudrāṇī, and Brahmāṇī (from left to right)

15. INDRĀṆĪ TEMPLE

This temple is located on the bank of the Viṣṇumati River near the bridge leading to the Svayambhū Stūpa. This pagoda-style temple has a wooden *toraṇa*, on which the Eight Mātṛkās are depicted.

Pl. 230 Indrāṇī Temple
Pl. 231 The *toraṇa* depicting the Eight Mātṛkās

Indrāṇī, who is represented here as the main deity among the Mātṛkās seen on the *toraṇa*, is flanked by the two terrifying goddesses, Cāmuṇḍā (right) and Vārāhī (left).

16. THE EIGHT MĀTṚKĀS ILLUSTRATED IN A MANUSCRIPT FOUND IN PATAN

I found the following illustrations of the Eight Mātṛkās in a manuscript. They are part of a private collection belonging to a man living in Patan. The contents of the manuscript concerns Mātṛkā rites.

Pl. 232 Brahmāyaṇī
Pl. 233 Māheśvarī
Pl. 234 Kaumārī
Pl. 235 Vaiṣṇavī
Pl. 236 Vārāhī
Pl. 237 Indrāyaṇī
Pl. 238 Cāmuṇḍā
Pl. 239 Nārasiṃhī

Here, Nārasiṃhī has been substituted for Mahālakṣmī. She is also sometimes substituted for Cāmuṇḍā.

17. THE EIGHT MĀTṚKĀS IN THE *DEVATĀCITRASAṂGRAHĀTMAKA*

The *Devatācitrasaṃgrahātmaka* published by Vīrapustaka Ālaya of Kathmandu contains about three hundred black and white drawings of Hindu deities.[32] The book seems to be one of the most systematic works of Nepalese Hindu iconography. The contents of the work are as follows:

Nos. 1-17:	Śiva
Nos. 18-55:	Viṣṇu
No. 56:	Brahmā
Nos. 57-86:	Śaktis
Nos. 87-100:	Siddhas and Gaṇas
Nos. 101-115:	Grahagaṇas (the sun, moon, and planets)
Nos. 116-127:	Nāgas (snakes)
Nos. 128-154:	Nakṣatras (stars)
Nos. 155-166:	Rāśis (zodiac constellations)
Nos. 167-174:	Digpālas (gurdians)
Nos. 175-189:	Viśvakarman, Kiṃnara, Preta, Vetāla, and Kṣetrapāla
Nos. 190-254:	Yoginīs and Bhairavas
Appendix Nos. 1 -63:	Yoginīs (mentioned in the *Devīpurāṇa*)
Illustrations 71-78:	Eight Mātṛkās, the female partners (*śaktis*) of various gods

Pl. 240 Brahmāṇī (*Devatācitrasaṃgrahātmaka* No. 71)
Pl. 241 Rudrāṇī (*ibid.* No. 72)

Pl. 242 Kaumārī, (*ibid.* No. 73)
Pl. 243 Vaiṣṇavī (*ibid.* No. 74)
Pl. 244 Vārāhī (*ibid.* No. 75)
Pl. 245 Indrāṇī (*ibid.* No. 76)
Pl. 246 Cāmuṇḍā (*ibid.* No. 77)
Pl. 247 Mahālakṣmī (*ibid.* No. 78)

18. THE EIGHT MĀTṚKĀS ILLUSTRATED ACCORDING TO THE *AṢṬAMĀTṚKĀSTOTRA*

The following Eight Mātṛkās have been painted by Mr. Gautama R. Vajracarya, a Nepalese artist who lives in Kathmandu. He was brought up in a traditional Newar family which belongs to the Buddhist community (*guṭhi*) called Mantrasiddhimahāvihāra.

Pl. 248 Brahmāyaṇī
Pl. 249 Raudrāyaṇī
Pl. 250 Indrāyaṇī
Pl. 251 Vārāhī
Pl. 252 Kaumārī
Pl. 253 Vaiṣṇavī
Pl. 254 Cāmuṇḍā
Pl. 255 Mahālakṣmī

The painter used the *Aṣṭamātṛkāstotra* (Hymn to the Eight Mātṛkās) as text for his illustrations. This hymn is recited nowadays during Buddhist worship services. The Sanskrit text of the hymn has been published by a religious group, but text is not entitled the *Aṣṭamātṛkāstotra*. Nonetheless, Newar Buddhists call this text by the name. The Sanskrit used in this text is greatly influenced by Newari language and does not follow the *sandhi* rules of classical Sanskrit in almost every line.

The first eight verses of the hymn have been assigned to the description of the Eight Mātṛkās: each verse describes each Mātṛkā. The first verse describes Brahmāyaṇī possessing a *kamaṇḍalu* pot. The second verse describes Raudrāyaṇī possessing a trident and a skull cup (*pātra*). The third one is about Indrāyaṇī possessing a *vajra*, and in the fourth verse, Vārāhī holds a fish and a hook. In this manner, Kaumārī, Vaiṣṇavī, Cāmuṇḍā, and Mahālakṣmī have also been described as possessing, respectively, a *śakti*, a *cakra*, a sword and a shield, and a skull cup (*kapāla*) and a sword. The text of the *Aṣṭamātṛkāstotra* runs as follows:

नमः अष्ट मातृका देव्यै

ब्रम्हायणी पीतवर्णाभा कमण्डलु धरं शुभाम् ।
वेदमाता विशालाक्षीं नमामि हंस वाहिनीम् ॥१॥

रौद्रायणी श्वेतवर्णाभा त्रिशूल पात्र धारिनीम् ।
त्रिनेत्रा चारु वदना नमामि वृप वाहिनीम् ॥२॥

इन्द्रा यणी कुम्कूमाङ्गी वज्रहस्ता सूरेश्वरीम् ।
सहस्र नयना सौम्यां नमामि गजवाहिनीम् ॥३॥

वाराही रक्तवर्णाभा मीनाङ्कुश धराशुभाम् ।
घन घोर कोलास्या नमामि महिष वाहिनीम् ॥४॥

कौमारी रक्तवर्णाभा शक्ति हस्ता भयानकीम् ।
त्रिनेत्रा योवनां गीच नमामि शिखिवाहिनीम् ॥५॥

वैष्णवी श्यामवर्णाभा चक्रहस्ता मनोहराम् ।
त्रिनेत्रा सौम्य वदनां नमामि गरुड वाहिनीम् ॥६॥

चामूण्डा रक्तवर्णाभा खड्ग फेटक धारिनीम् ।
कृष्णाङ्गी क्रोध रुपाच नमामि प्रेत वाहिनीम् ॥७॥

महालक्ष्मी श्वेतवर्णा कपाल खड्ग धारिनीम् ॥
त्रिनेत्रा सौम्य वदनां नमामि सिंह वाहिनीम् ॥८॥

अष्ट क्षत्रे स्थितादेवी अष्ट वृक्ष निवासिनीम् ।
अष्ट भैरव संयुक्तं अष्ट मातृकां नमस्तुते ॥९॥

असिताङ्गं प्रचण्डं च रुरुकं कपिलं तथा ।
क्रोध उन्मत्त संहारं भीपम भैरवं नमः ॥१०॥

गणनां गणपति श्चैव गज वक्रं त्रिलोचनं ।
परशु मोदक हस्तं च गणपति नमोस्तुते ॥११॥

वीर विक्रम सौन्दर्य्यं शक्ति हस्तन्तु षट्मुखम्
सर्व सिद्धि प्रदातारं कुमार प्रनमाम्यऽहम् ॥१२।

स्वस्थानं स्वधिकारं च स्वस्वरूप स्व वीजजम् ।
स्वस्व काष्ट वितानं च दिव्याना कुञ्ज भूमिकम् ॥१३॥

दश दिशु क्षत्रपालं क्षत्राश्चैव त्रयोदश
पञ्चा शत क्षत्र पालाश्च क्षत्र पालं नमस्तुते ॥१४।

(Vadrīratna Vajrācārya, Fine Art Printing Press, Vaṭu Cikaṃat, 1970)

19. THE EIGHT MĀTṚKĀS ILLUSTRATED BY A NEPALESE PAINTER

The following illustrations (Pl. 256-263) were drawn by a Nepalese painter named Mr. Ishwar Karmacarya. He followed his own imaginations while drawing the Mātṛkās, and did not refer to any particular text of the time.

Pl. 256 Brahmāṇī
Pl. 257 Rudrāṇī
Pl. 258 Kaumārī
Pl. 259 Vaiṣṇavī
Pl. 260 Vārāhī
Pl. 261 Indrāṇī
Pl. 262 Cāmuṇḍā
Pl. 263 Mahālakṣmī

As usual, the characteristic symbols of the Mātṛkās are found in the second left hand of each Mātṛkā. A hook is Brahmāṇī's symbol; a trident, Rudrāṇī's symbol; a *śakti*, Kumāra's symbol; and a *khaṭvāṅga*, Mahālakṣmī's symbol. All are found in a left hand of these four Mātṛkās; the right hand of each of these four Mātṛkās holds a rosary. The remaining four Mātṛkās, however, hold their characteristic symbols in both hands. Vaiṣṇavī holds a club and a *cakra*, which are two important symbols of both Viṣṇu and Vaiṣṇavī. Vārāhī has a fish and a hook; Indrāṇī has an umbrella and a *vajra*; Cāmuṇḍā holds a shield and a sword.

20. THE EIGHT MĀTṚKĀS IN THE VAJRAVĀRĀHĪ MAṆḌALA

The Eight Mātṛkās sometimes appear in Buddhist Maṇḍalas, especially in Newar Buddhist Maṇḍalas. For example, the Eight Mātṛkās together with the Eight Bhairabs appear in the Vajravārāhī Maṇḍala, which is well known in the Kathmandu Valley. The tantric Goddess Vajravārāhī is found in the inverted triangle symbolizing the *dharmodayā*, from which the primordial matter developed into universe. The combination of the inverted and vertical triangles represents union. Female energy is symbolized by the inverted triangle, and male energy is symbolized by the vertical one. The Eight Mātṛkās and the Eight Bhairabs are found in the outer circle of the Maṇḍala.

This Maṇḍala has been drawn by Mr. Gautama R. Vajracarya, who has also illustrated the Eight Mātṛkās according to the *Aṣṭamātṛkāstotra*

Figure 15 Vajravārāhī Maṇḍala

(cf. Pl. 248-255). The names of the deities that appear in the Maṇḍala are as follows:

No. 1 Vajravārāhī
No. 2 Ḍākinī
No. 3 Lāmā
No. 4 Khaṇḍarohā
No. 5 Rūpiṇī
No. 6 Vārāhī
No. 7 Phaṭphaṭcandikā
No. 8 Saṃtrāsinī
No. 9 Saṃcāriṇī
No. 10 Mohinī
No. 11 Yāminī
No. 12 Brahmāyaṇī

No. 13 Asitāṅgabhairava
No. 14 Kaumārī
No. 15 Krodhabhairava
No. 16 Vārāhī
No. 17 Pracaṇḍabhairava
No. 18 Vaiṣṇavī
No. 19 Ulmantabhairava
No. 20 Indrāyaṇī
No. 21 Rurukabhairava
No. 22 Cāmuṇḍā
No. 23 Saṃhārabhairava
No. 24 Rudrāyaṇī
No. 25 Kapālabhairava
No. 26 Mahālakṣmī
No. 27 Bhīṣaṇabhairava

The arrangement of the Eight Mātṛkās according to these Buddhist sects is different from that of those Hindu temples such as Bhadra Kālī and Hadigaon Bhavagatī temples. It is probably because the Maṇḍala is originally belonging to the Buddhist tradition. The following Mātṛkās were drawn by Mr. Gautama R. Vajracarya and his brother Mr. Sarvajña Vajracarya.

Pl. 264 Vajravārāhī Maṇḍala
Pl. 265 Brahmāyaṇī
Pl. 266 Kaumārī
Pl. 267 Vārāhī[33)]
Pl. 268 Vaiṣṇavī
Pl. 269 Indrāyaṇī
Pl. 270 Cāmuṇḍā
Pl. 271 Rudrāyaṇī
Pl. 272 Mahālakṣmī

ABBREVIATION

KV=*Kathmandu Valley*, ed. by C. Pruscha, 1975.

NOTES

1) This temple is not mentioned in *KV*. For its location, see *Kathmandu City* 1:10,000. 8 colours, Nepal-Kartenwerk der Arbeitsgemeinschaft fuer vergleichende Hochgebirgsforschung, Nr. 21, 9-H.
2) *KV*, Vol. 2, 1975: 54; B/K-149; van Kooij, K. R. 1978: 17.
3) *KV*, Vol. 2, 1975: 54.
4) Usually, a Mātṛkā is drawn mounted on a vehicle; but here, instead, are two buffalos, two geese, etc.
5) K. R. van Kooij calls this deity Durgā (van Kooij, K. R. 1978: Pl. X1Xb).
6) Here a peaceful form and a wrathful form of Śiva are depicted. Bhairab (Skt., Bhairava) is a wrathful form of Śiva.
7) *KV*, Vol. 2, 1975: 164; A/P-130; Slusser, M. 1982: Pl. 127; Majupuria, T. C. and Majupuria, I. 1979-1980: 194. Cf. Korn, W.1976: Fig. 24; Fujioka, M. and Watanabe, K. 1981: Fig. 7.
8) *KV*, Vol. 2, 1975: 63; B/K-177; Wiesner, U. 1976: 57.
9) *KV*, Vol. 2, 1975: 102; B/K-301.
10) Majupuria, T. C. and Majupuria, I. 1979-1980: 48.
11) G.Tucci presented several photographs of the frescoes (Tucci, G. 1968: 166). Cf. Tachikawa 990: 246-251.
12) Slusser, M. 1982: Pl. 517; Tachikawa 1990: 256.
13) Tachikawa, M. 1983: 123.
14) *KV*, Vol. 2, 1975: 176; B/P-171.
15) The names of the Bhairabs appearing in Plates 96, 102, 104, and 108 are inscribed at the bottom of each strut. The Bhairab shown in Pl. 94 is probably Ruru Bhairab, because he holds a *vīṇā* in his left hand (cf. Gupte, R. S. 1972: 76).
16) *KV*, Vol. 1, 1975: 146, no. 6.
17) Majupuria, T.C., and Majupuria, I, 1979-1980: 30.
18) *KV*, Vol. 2, 1975: 133; B/P-10.
19) *KV*, Vol. 2, 1975: 177; B/P-175.
20) *KV*, Vol. 2, 1975: 177.
21) *KV*, Vol. 2, 1975: 105; C/K-304.
22) To give another example, there is a relief of an iguana at the main entrance of the Taleju Temple, Bhadgaon (cf. *KV*, Vol. 2, 1975: 217: A/B-8).
23) *KV*, Vol. 2, 1975: 97; B/K-286.
24) Majupuria, T. C. and Majupuria, I. 1979-1980: 139.

25) Krishna Sastri 1974: 197.
26) *KV*, Vol. 2, 1975: 103; C/K-307.
27) This stone idol is believed to have been made in the 8th or 9th century (Slusser M. 1982: Pl. 418).
28) *KV*, Vol. 2, 1975: 162; A/P-126.
29) Majupuria, T. C. and Majupuria, I. 1979-1980: 194-195. As for the Large Taleju Temple, see *ibid.* 192-193.
30) *KV*, Vol. 1, 1975: 184; V-MZ21 .
31) *KV*, Vol. 2, 1975: 14: C/K-13.
32) Bāvukṛṣṇa 1962; Bühnemamn and Tachikawa 1990.
33) Tachikawa, M. 1987: 107.

BIBLIOGRAPHY

Bāvukṛṣṇa
1962 *Devatācitrasaṃgrahātmaka*, Vīrapustaka Ālaya, Kathmandu.

Bühnemamn, G. and Tachikawa, M.
1990 *The Hindu Deities Illustrated*, The Centre for East Asian Cultural Studies for Unesco, The Toyo Bunko, Tokyo.

Fujioka, M. and Watanabe, K.
1981 *The Royal Building in Nepal*, Nippon Institute of Technology, Research Mission.

Gupte, R.S.
1972 *Iconography of the Hindus Buddhists and Jains*, D.B.Taraporevala Sons & Co. Private Ltd., Bombay.

Jung, C.G.
1986 *Four Archetypes*, Art Paperbacks, London/ New York.

Korn, W.
1976 *The Traditional Architecture of the Kathmandu Valley*, Ratna Pustak Bhandar, Kathmandu.

Krishna Shāstri, H.
1974 *South-Indian Images of Gods and Goddesses*, Bharatiya Publishing House, Delhi.

Majupuria, T. C. and Majupuria, I.
1979-80 *Glimpses of Nepal*, Smt. Maha Devī, Lalitpur.

Pruscha, C.
1975 *Kathmandu Valley. The Preservation or Physical Environment and Culture Heritage: A Protective Inventory (2 vols.)*, Anton Scroll & Co. Publishers, Vienna.

Shastri, J. L. (ed.)
1973 *Brahmāṇḍa Purāṇa*, Motilal Banarsidass, New Delhi.

Slusser, M.
1982 *Nepal Mandala*, Princeton University Press, Princeton, New Jersey, 2 vols.
Tachikawa, M.
1978 "Kathmandu no Naksāl Bahgavatī-ji" (Naksāl Bhagavatī in Kathmandu), *YAK* , Institute for the Study of Languages and Cultures of Asia and Africa, No. 2, pp.1-25, Tokyo.
1983 "Kathmandu no kamigami" (Deities in Kathmandu), *Kikan Minzokugaku*, Minzokugaku Shinkokai, No. 26, pp.114-124.
1984 "Materials for Iconographic Studies of the Eight Mother-Goddesses in the Kathmandu Valley", Part 1: Plates. *Anthropological and Linguistic Studies of the Gandaki Area in Nepal (Monumenta Serindica*, No. 12), Institute for the Study of Languages and Cultures of Asia and Africa, pp.1-122, Tokyo.
1985 ibid., Part I-2, pp.41-116.
1986 "Kathmandu ni okeru Hachiboshin to Hachibairaba" (The Eight Mātṛkās and the Eight Bhairavas in Kathmandu), The Mikkyo Zuzo (*Iconography of Esoteric Buddhism*), No. 4 , pp.22-38.
1987 *Mandara no Kamigami* (*Maṇḍala Deities*), Arina Shobō, Tokyo.
1990 *Nyoshintachi no Indo* (*India of Goddesses*), Serika Publishing Co., Tokyo.
Tucci, G.
1968 Lati Līlā, tr. by J. Hogarth, Nagel Publishers, Geneva-Paris-Munich.
Vadrīratna Vajrācārya
1970 [*Aṣṭamātṛkāstotra*], Fine Art Printing Press, Vatu Cikamat, Kathmandu.
Van Kooij, K. R.
1978 *Religion in Nepal*, Institute of Religions Iconography, State University Groningen, Leiden E. J. Brill.
Wiesner, U.
1976 *Nepal, Königreich im Himalaya, Geschichte, Kunst und Kultur im Kathmandu-Tal*, Du Mont Kunst-Reiseführer.

Pl. 1

Pl. 2

Pl. 3

P*l*. 4

P*l*. 5

P*l*. 6

P*l*. 7

Pl. 8

Pl. 9

Pl. 10

Pl. 11

P*l*. 12

Pl. 13

Pl. 14

Pl. 15

Pl. 16

Pl. 17

Pl. 18

Pl. 19

Pl. 20

Pl. 21

Pl. 22

Pl. 23

Pl. 24

Pl. 25

Pl. 26

Pl. 27

Pl. 28

Pl. 29

Pl. 30

P*l.* 31

P*l.* 32

Pl. 33

Pl. 34

Pl. 35

Pl. 36

Pl. 37

Pl. 38

Pl. 39

Pl. 40

Pl. 41

Pl. 42

Pl. 43

Pl. 44

Pl. 45

Pl. 46

Pl. 47

Pl. 48

Pl. 49

Pl. 50

Pl. 51

Pl. 52

Pl. 53

Pl. 54

Pl. 55

Pl. 56

Pl. 57

Pl. 58

Pl. 59

Pl. 60

Pl. 61

Pl. 62

Pl. 63

Pl. 64

Pl. 65

Pl. 66

Pl. 69

Pl. 70

Pl. 71

Pl. 72

Pl. 73

Pl. 74

Pl. 75

Pl. 76

Pl. 77

Pl. 78

Pl. 79

Pl. 80

Pl. 81

Pl. 82

Pl. 83

Pl. 84

Pl. 85

Pl. 86

Pl. 87

Pl. 88

Pl. 89

Pl. 90

Pl. 91

Pl. 92

Pl. 93

Pl. 94

Pl. 95

Pl. 96

Pl. 97

Pl. 98

Pl. 99

Pl. 100

Pl. 101

Pl. 102

Pl. 103

Pl. 104

Pl. 105

Pl. 106

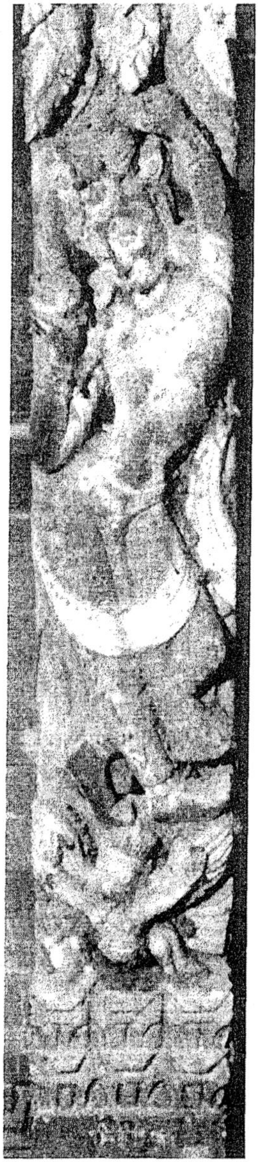

Pl. 107

Pl. 108

Pl. 109

Pl. 110

Pl. 111

Pl. 112

Pl. 113

Pl. 114

Pl. 115

Pl. 116

Pl. 117

Pl. 118

Pl. 119

Pl. 120

Pl. 121

Pl. 122

Pl. 123

Pl. 124

Pl. 125

Pl. 126

Pl. 127

Pl. 128

Pl. 129

Pl. 13

Pl. 131

Pl. 132

Pl. 133

Pl. 134

Pl. 135

Pl. 136

Pl. 137

Pl. 138

Pl. 139

Pl. 140

Pl. 141

Pl. 142

Pl. 143

Pl. 144

Pl. 145

Pl. 146

Pl. 147

Pl. 148

Pl. 149

Pl. 150

Pl. 151

Pl. 152

Pl. 153

Pl. 154

Pl. 155

Pl. 156

Pl. 157

Pl. 158

Pl. 159

Pl. 160

Pl. 161

Pl. 162

Pl. 163

Pl. 164

Pl. 165

Pl. 166

Pl. 167

Pl. 168

Pl. 169

Pl. 170

Pl. 171

Pl. 172

Pl. 173

Pl. 174

Pl. 175

Pl. 176

Pl. 177

Pl. 178

Pl. 179

Pl. 180

Pl. 181

Pl. 182

Pl. 183

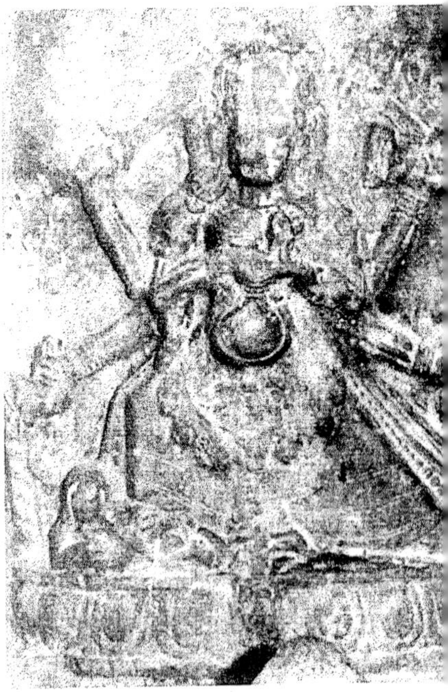

Pl. 184

Pl. 185

Pl. 186

Pl. 187

Pl. 188

Pl. 189

Pl. 190

Pl. 191

Pl. 192

Pl. 193

Pl. 194

Pl. 195

Pl. 196

Pl. 197

P*l.* 198

Pl. 199

P*l*. 200

P*l*. 201

P*l*. 202

P*l*. 203

P*l*. 204

P*l*. 205

P*l*. 206

P*l*. 207

Pl. 208

Pl. 209

Pl. 210

Pl. 211

Pl. 212

Pl. 213

Pl. 214

Pl. 215

Pl. 216

Pl. 217

Pl. 218

Pl. 219

Pl. 220

Pl. 221

Pl. 222

Pl. 223

Pl. 224

Pl. 225

Pl. 226

Pl. 227

Pl. 228

Pl. 229

Pl. 230

Pl. 231

Pl. 232

Pl. 233

Pl. 234

Pl. 235

Pl. 236

Pl. 237

Pl. 238

Pl. 239

ब्रह्माणी गौरवर्णा

Pl. 240

रुद्राणी श्वेतवर्णा

Pl. 241

कौमारी रक्तवर्णा

Pl. 242

वैष्णवी श्यामवर्णा

Pl. 243

वाराही तरुणी श्यामवर्णा

Pl. 244

इन्द्राणी त्रिनेत्रा कुङ्कुमवर्णा

Pl. 245

चामुण्डा श्यामवर्णा

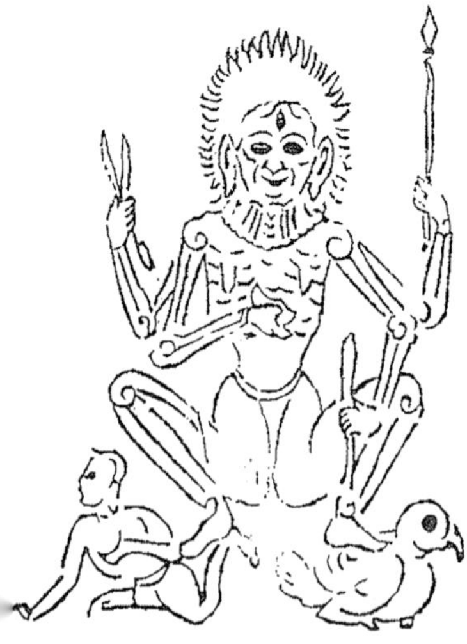

Pl. 246

महालक्ष्मी श्यामवर्णा

Pl. 247

Pl. 248

Pl. 249

Pl. 250

Pl. 251

Pl. 252

Pl. 253

Pl. 254

Pl. 255

Pl. 256

Pl. 257

Pl. 258

Pl. 259

Pl. 260

Pl. 261

Pl. 262

Pl. 263

Pl. 264

श्रीब्रम्हायणी

Pl. 265

श्री कौमारी

Pl. 266

श्री वाराही

Pl. 267

P*l*. 268

श्री ऐन्द्रायणी

Pl. 269

श्रीचामुण्डा

Pl. 270

श्रीरुद्रायणी

P*l*. 271

श्री माहालक्ष्मी

Pl. 272